TRUE FORENSICS

Ken Evans can zone in on words so that they almost
hurt, registering emotional as well as physical damage:
in poems as strong as 'The Train Rushes to us with
Precious Gifts from Far-Away ', he shows us what it is
to take seemingly ordinary words, 'since' and 'stroke',
and charge them with new significance.

But Evans is also a poet with a scientific bent, who likes
to register the facts of a situation and then test them
in memorable poems like 'The Fallen Snow' and in
carefully plotted, self-scrutinizing lines like these from
'Jet-lag in Ocean Gardens, British Columbia', which
observing the world as it is, and also our insistent
attempts to come to terms with it, notices: 'the snapper
who steps across my view / of the ocean, holding up
his Nikon by way of apology, / my sight-line arrested,
the slide-show of white light / over Greenland, from
what was last night.'
JOHN McAULIFFE

TRUE FORENSICS

KEN EVANS

POETRY

 EYEWEAR PUBLISHING

First published in 2018
by Eyewear Publishing Ltd
Suite 333, 19-21 Crawford Street
Marylebone, London W1H 1PJ
United Kingdom

Cover design and typeset by Edwin Smet

Printed in England by TJ International Ltd, Padstow, Cornwall

ISBN 978-1-912477-10-4

WWW.EYEWEARPUBLISHING.COM

Ken Evans won the 2018 Kent & Sussex Poetry Competition and
The Battered Moons Competition in 2016. He was included in
an anthology of *Best New British & Irish Poets*, edited by
Luke Kennard. Kennard referred to his featured poem as 'a
hypnotic exercise in imagination and compassion.' Evans'
first pamphlet, *The Opposite of Defeat*, featured work from his
shortlisted collection in The Poetry School's / Nine Arches
Press 'Primers' Competition, which also shortlisted in
Bare Fiction's debut competition. *True Forensics* is his
debut full poetry collection.

TABLE OF CONTENTS

STOPPING FOR CHIPS

Walking back from an Everton result at midnight,
a graveyard slab, the bench of choice to finish chips.
The security-light on the church picks out our wrappers,
slickened by vinegar, dewy with salt; the bored audience
of a theatre under brown headstones, pint-glasses
with flat-heads. A trickle of moonlight in the yew,
the old red heartwood, the new white sapwood,
blood and body, body and blood, as our open mouths,
between two lights, savour the grease, the heat.

DOWN AT THE LEISURE CENTRE

The tongue of an ewe licks
the lamb of my chest
into life: two beige pads
take the pre-set volts,
jolting my heart
from the bounded chamber.
A computerised voice
asks the bystander to light me up,
as they help till 'Help' is here.

Compressions:
In, Out – Charge!
Flat hands push me down
and bring me back.
My eyes open on the heaven
of a Leisure Centre,
where members kick off death
in webbed trainers.
The defib. keeps me on
an inside track,
taking tight corners,
till the ambulance crew,
their tough-guy humour and orange neck-brace,
say what a perfect spot
to be arrested.

EN FEMME

I gave up drugs when the wig arrived, stopped drawing
the curtains to wear a dress. I'd leave a make-up bag
by the front-door, half-hoping inappropriate callers

catch me, after work, doing my face, in the mirror,
inexpertly at first, then with class and Cyndi Lauper
cranked up loud. I'd teeter to the drive and back

in purple-heels, bought online from *Janet's Closet*. Giddy,
as I wore a satin jacquard bustier with cotton blouse,
the first time: no-one registered, or else they smirked

behind their hands. A sling-shot gaff flattens an unsightly
bulge out-front; panty-hose to smooth hairs on the leg,
fur against my thighs, cool over junkyard genitals.

My calves, their beautiful profile in big heels.
I was the quiet guy on the corner whose wife left
one morning, the roles in a marriage dissolved.

I studied hard my bras; learnt long about hip-sway
and breast forms, yearning for the moonish of a period,
the way time counts down through all of us.

THE LIST OF THINGS YOU LOSE IF YOU KILL YOURSELF BEFORE SIXTY

No, Sidhak, it doesn't make it better
you would be sixty this year, eligible

for a Senior Rail card, cheap days-out,
free buses (as a Londoner), Cold Weather

payments on income-based Jobseekers'
Allowance, a free eye test and prescriptions,

all that you opted out of; SERPS, a pensionable
step too far, you dead these thirty years:

a memory of a call from a friend down
the bright day's line, saying you killed yourself

in Norway, as if the 'where' mattered,
and I, unused to loss like any complacent,

asked: 'How?'
as if, Sidhak, method was important.

You've no benefits, or rights to be here,
still haunting, because we lost you and didn't go

back the way we came
to find you, the brambled path,

no rights at all, to swing from a tree as if
this, the brightest lantern you could swing

at life. 'You can't speak ill of the dead,'
friends say, but what if the dead make me ill?

Being alone with you,
a spectre, as you know full well, Sid,

your grip stays firm as each year hangs
weights off us; all the things you didn't do,

the things we did. The clothes your wife
gave me, washed and pressed, I couldn't send

to charity, though as they spun from my arms
they seemed to resurrect you, spontaneously,

fill out their crumpledness, as they fell
in a bin-liner – jumpers, jeans, shirts –

jiggled like on the end of a rope.
I tied a top-knot on that black plastic bag,

the sash of your lustrous, perpendicular hair.

THE TRAIN RUSHES TO US WITH PRECIOUS GIFTS FROM FAR AWAY

Since, I have to think harder
what I say. Words are pond carp
who, on sipping at the surface,
gobble their own sound.

Since, a nail is harder to hit,
the weight of the hammer-head
needs thought not to shatter
the wood or curl the nail.

Since, I slur, by which I mean,
I'm tired, by which I mean, a part
of my brain is gone; I mean,
I'm losing the light. Soft synapses.

Stroke means to caress gently,
a butterfly applying pressure
to a petal. To stoke is to build-up
from a little. A streak is clouds.

THE DETECTORISTS

Earphones earthed to a field,
dial a past that's engaged,
or is reverting to voicemail; a blip,
a halo-sound from magnetite,
hematite, iron residue in the ground.

Done not for a golden handful of soil,
nor a swing of the pendant, a buzzing
in the ears, but for that second before
the lip takes the hook, and declares
it bullion, a ring-pull, or nail.

Not for the money, fame, or glory,
only to listen out for something more
than the incline of your own
breathing, the pleasure a fish
feels on breaking the surface.

HILL-WALKING IN THE BRECON BEACONS

not right now
          pouring the last
of your personality into the worn
          ear of the nurse;

falling through your one good eye
          to meet the car
exiting you at a junction;

nor found cold, slumped
          on the bowl, the least
warm thing among condensation;

definitely not face-down in a hall,
          a hard edge
of furniture thick to your skull;

because for now, the future rolls
          to a big blue ball,
you pulling up a green hill

          red fists clinging
to springy-kneed bilberry bushes
          not yet cropping;

the sun a saucer of milk
          balanced on your neck,
the last false summit curving

          to a final brown top,
your heart
          hammering, the lick.

LONTANO

Eyes half-sunk in mud, a hagfish, in its spineless chest, senses fear
as vibration, his own horny-tooth suckers sifting sand, and knows no fear.

A single note travels archipelagos of sound, turns in watery fingers;
like Di Caprio in the empty ward on *Shutter Island*, we fear the worst.

The composer-refugee, under mail-bags in a truck as tanks rumble in '56,
hears the tremor in his heart through the sackcloth, calves tight with fear.

A flute raises hairs on your neck, the foreboding of a slave-camp worker,
knowing that to give in means a shovel for you too, no flight from terror.

Signal from a NASA probe, a pulse searching for anyone out there
who understands our planet of jagged violins, the quavering of our fears.

A house you return to in the dark, the imprint of a stranger's footprint,
a chair bumped into that you did not move; behind you, a creeping fear.

I take an age, it seems, to suck the sweet globe of a grape in my mouth
till the skin explodes, and juice spills from my lips in a fearless, red ribbon.

THE FIRE IN THE HEARTH

Screams of expulsion
        from the bedroom,
            feet chase the stairs down,

a warm red sludge seeping through
        a *Sunday Mirror* turns
            auntie's forearms orange,

her pinafore lurid. She strides to the fire
        as we watch, volume raised,
            The Man from U.N.C.L.E..

A marlin out of water, hook-hung,
        flopping to the hearth,
            a red delta and a milky cord,

the lightning-flash over a scarlet sunset,
        the flame-fattening placenta,
            all heft and coil,

the waterless slab of it,
        blue and bloody, boiling
            in the grate.

To help and hold back tears, I riddle
        what's left in an ash-pan,
            walk it down the garden,

flakes trapping in my knuckle-hair
        as I tip grey piles
            on a compost-heap,

wonder at the squeezed, red folds
of my little brother's face
after the fire.

THE SPICE FESTIVAL

In the dark house of longing, fling wide
each door, throw light from a landing
over unvarnished skirting-boards:
a bathroom, a twist of a shower-head,
bhandara rubbed to sunshine colour
between splayed fingers in the spray,
Jejuri Temple rising in the steam:

jiggery and herb pancakes, turmeric
bangles tied to our wrists by the faithful,
the sky powdered gold, our eyelashes
like a bee's back, sticky with pollen,
the moon through the trees
making cracks in the sky.

TIR A' MHACHAIR, TIR NAN LOCH

Gaelic: Land of the Machair, Land of Water

On Cairngorm, a new glacier tongue wags,
unlike the shrivelled silences of Alaska;
Glasgow barely above zero in winter, icicles
hang from a child's mobile in a pushchair;
on Uist, the machair sunken, and come
summer, the Great Yellow Bumble-Bee,

fingered by the Mexican Wave of a jet
stream's swerve, feels an onshore breeze
cool his last known address, loses his shoes
to the drowned red clover, where once
there was dancing; the black stripe on
the gold back, a bar-code binary of gone,

or surviving. The lapwing's *pee-wit-wit*,
the call of a dunlin, are drowned out
by breakers hurled at saline lagoons
along the Howmore's eddying course:
only the salt-encrusted stonewort
shines, cold and hard.

LEARNING FINNISH PROVERBS

One cannot ski so softly the tracks are not seen:
more lakes than people, and the forest wraps
their riffled contours, a fur-coat on a model.
Moose scat, pine scent. Shop for a month
for the cabin, for the tsunami of Auroran night
engulfs, though here in the Kingdom of Nokia,
the wider the desert, the better the wifi,
Ei kannata mennä merta edemmäs kalaan:

It is not worth going further than the sea for fish.
A wood-stove in a forest, asking the question
'Why do people matter?' On snow-chains to
The Northern Lights Pizza & Disco, a high-stool,
and a grizzled old-timer with stories of survival,
a telecoms engineer, feeding the clapping seal
of the juke-box, 'Don't You Want Me, Baby,'
on repeat: *Accidents don't have a bell on their neck.*

The barman wipes the night with an oily towel,
smearing the stars, like midges, on a window.
The music blocks the sound of falling snow, creaking
to a tipping-point; we are buried, tipsy and alive,
till the iron grin of the snow-plough breaks through
the white dream of morning. I don't recall the lyrics,
but the 'Ala viitsi!' *(No way!)* of the publican,
with three bars on his phone, scrolling for rescue:

Ei pidä tehdä kärpäsestä härkää.
One shouldn't make a bull out of a fly.

ÖTZI THE ICEMAN

If you must die, even five thousand years ago, there were worse spots:
under an earlier sun, it could end in a viburnum-quiver arrow
to the chest, the stab of an ibex horn, or starved of fish you cannot
hoick from the lake, and months to pass till the berry-season.

Here, in a col between snowy alps, a fall of black and yellow rock,
covered by inedible, gorgeous lichen; a mound of wind-whipped
grass on which to sit and take your breath, your stomach turning
from the altitude, and the whip-worm in your gut.

The only salve is birch fungi, a full pouch at your neck,
the leather, taut as a wire, still sings in an alpine blast,
the brown daggers of your clavicles, ice-crystals in the eyes
like fallen fragments from the last stars you saw.

The mushroom, as well-preserved as your toe-nails and hair; useful
when dry, for sharpening the flint they found beside you, the rasp
of a stropped edge in blue air, the clear echo off a rock wall.

ON FINDING COLD SPOTS

If not as warm
as once you were,
check your radiators.
Bubbles make cold spots
in your system. Free
the trapped air.
Turn up your heat,
let the pressure rise,
and force air out.
If you find cold spots,
switch off; cold spots
in your radiator, a sure
sign air is caught.
Bleed out, bleed out.

You'll need a key, or a flat-end
screwdriver does as well.
At a corner of your unit,
find the valve, attach the key
or slot the screwdriver
in the groove. Hold a cloth
to catch your drips. Turn the key
or screwdriver anti-
clockwise, listen for a hiss:
once air's expelled, water flows.
Close-off to avoid a spurt.
Check pressure on the gauge.

If you're low, top up, top up.
Use the tap on your boiler
called the filling loop.

Test your own success. Turn
on your heat once more, wait
till the system is hot to touch.
Once you're sweating,
check for cold spots like a vet
feels a calf-stomach for tumours.
If you find one, repeat as above,
and bleed out, bleed out.
If this doesn't work, call for help,
though no-one knows more
about your radiators than you.

HOMEOPATHIC

Six weeks' heat, which for Derbyshire is news.
Mirages criss-cross the bleached garden, the lightest
breeze a brown crackle in the hedge, and shrubs quiver
in a border, like morning shoulders putting on an overcoat.
Leaves jerk their wire branches back across the green dance-
floor where they came from, spilling light at every twist,
lessening the pressure on the forehead.

ON COLLEGE ROAD

A black case stands
to attention by the stairs.
I only pack what training
has found acceptable.

In the most sensible shoes
for my destination, I play
football with my nephew,
kick him the ball repeatedly.

Each pass is a bind, tying
us, his last goal cheered
as if fame and glory
sat under our goalposts.

Birds make decisions in trees.
Her dog, who never took
to me, my absence on tour,
still has faith I may walk him.

The taxi toots. I wipe dog-dribble
from best jeans. Years of service
lend familiarity; departures
to desert, exploded road.

I kiss my sister, her mix of worry
and relief at my being called back
to base, nights on her sofa. Today,
she can't say it won't be forever.

At the seminary gate, I say
drive on to the coastal road,
where that other eternal
chants vespers on the shingle.

This sense of presence, shadow
on an adobe wall; radio-crackle.
Cormorants spear a mirror of sea,
a carob pod against famine.

'THE NYMPHS ARE DEPARTED'

Eliot has them gone in favour of sandwich-wrappers, spent train-tickets,
coffee-receipts from hoped-for meetings with clients that never took place;
scratch-cards we lost at, and with no coin to rub, used dirty nails instead;
fag-butts and cider plastic, the unread instructions of condoms.

A river-bank, to spy for them in the unlooked-for, a white ripple on a rock
that winks back at you, a star in the night of your eyelid; a green reed
wriggling in a current, a fish, octopus, dugong or mermaid, turning
back into itself as you look again; the broken bark of a lime tree, a delta

unvisited, but recalled from an atlas. A pale-throated warbler bobs
above the water, the rufous tail flips light into red cash. A spider-web
strung across the honeying is a stretchy costume, hung on bushes
to get dry, that they never came back for, after a last dip in the sunshine.

THE TURN

Deliveroo cycles weave the flats, dark with revision
at midday, curtained. A face, lit like a pearl, peers
from the clam-shell of a lap-top. The Library is popular,
and some tutors sought-after as life-jackets in a flood,
surrounded by the soldier-ants who haul in silent,
grinding jaws the green leaves of unopened books.

A first tap of a beak breaks the bloom of a shell,
as what's about to begin is also a leaf-litter end,
the world poised between excitement and treachery.
Birds pick at blossom, tiny pink coracles of hope.
A breeze flattens a shirt to a chest, white papers
flutter in gymnasium air-con, waiting a turn.

WHITE HOLES IN THE WALLS

as if the insurgents have already won, looted the gallery,
shot the attendants against the walls, and left bullet-holes
in the blue; or the smashing of our own dam was foretold,
and art-handlers remove the canvases to higher ground
for safety: such holes, plastered smooth, where once hung
paintings of our decay, our every remission and relapse.
On the new curator's sign, inside perspex, it says
that white is freedom from our body, and the mind.

Drawing mental lines between the marks, we lose
the contours of a shape or object, slip to simpler forms
of difference: some blotches are just bigger in the sky.
They smash what they don't like and we, the people,
buy cards of these remedial planets in refurbished
gift-shops, with a fresh currency of bloody handkerchiefs,
seek out the spots on a wall for proof of how all our
previous choices fell into one black hole.

WITH 10 MINUTES TO CLOSING AT GoMA

I
a papier-mâché so white, you can't call the paper hair
on the mannequin, blonde; the dummy in black combats
and t-shirt, reads on her stomach, on a towel at the beach.
Beside her, as common as sun-screen, the black stock
and loaded magazine of her AK-47, fragrant violence.

II
a short film of a swarthy guy, shaved and ointmented:
a dark dress, his thighs stretch the tight material for a perfect
visual, back-strap shoes slip on with the twist of the hips
used for nothing else but sliding on hard-to-wear heels,
his mouth puckered to a carmine anus.

III
breeze-blocks to sight a gun through: African-mask heads
on top of the wall, three of them, bloodied, a grinning rictus.
Scarlet capes like emperors of a death-cult. Notes at the side
say this symbolic wall of Northernness is a black guy's feeling
of being imprisoned, even impaled, by Yorkshire blokeyness.

IV
Waterstones on Argyle Street: coffee and poetry, though the pages
don't turn; a woman humming, glasses high on her bridge, in a pose
of what reading must be like had we never heard of it. Is her song
drawing attention to herself or deflecting it? Is she inviting talk,
or waving us away? I know nothing of art.

THE WEIGHT-LOSS OF ENCOURAGEMENT

What if the great mystery is no big deal?
Apply only a lower burden of proof, as in
a belief in ghosts or animals, now extinct,
who come back to us in dreams, populate

our wallpaper, and breathe on our eyelids
at night: Heaven may be just this – pulling up
rungs of a blue sky, bird-song down to one
chirrup, the echo of each faltering step,

and our one competent god, backlit by sun,
with Renaissance halo, descends in Piero light
and air-flow Jack Wolfskin, a twenty metre
height advantage, brushstroking the mountain

with an outstretch of her walking-sticks,
a child-cherub at each swinging hip, who says,
with polite condescension, that I'll be on top in
only an hour, if I just keep plodding, plodding.

THE PLACING ON OF HANDS

Two hands touching at all times,
leading the steps of a dance.
Feet astride, watchful of hooves,
the right-hand at the stifle,
alert for the sign of a kick.

Work the flank, gaskin, hock,
the undertow of muscle,
a gravel beach, hissing down
the single, surgical tool
of your left-hand fingers,

pressuring the haunch, nickering
soothed with a slap to the croup:
the horse fears nothing but a lack
of confidence. The mane's coarse
cable tremors in your fist.

The sun filters through slats
of a barn; working round
your animal, the light, a shutter
opening and closing, a glow
in your fingers as they dig.

PARTY-BULBS

'I hate when your dreams treat you as stupid,'
grab the simplest things to upend you, dreams
not renowned for their even-handedness.

Hurl a big rock in their flow, they gulp it down,
a grey tip showing in summer, your dreams
lichening at the temples.

Build a dam like any good beaver, from twigs
of home, work, and relationship, dreams
splinter the construct, just the same.

A kind of patronising. You are bunting
in a downpour, your dreams, loose connections
in the party-bulbs, hung in the exulting dark.

SWEET TEA

What do you get if you swallow Tipp-Ex?
White poo. A gleam on an x-ray of the gut,
a dark tunnel before a blanket snow.

Does the junior tell the boss
it's the whitener in his coffee?
The manager goes home with cramps.

The taxi the boy calls for him doesn't show,
the number erased from the Contacts list
on his mobile.

Even clouds are an absence, holes
in a blue canvas. Online keyboard-killers
swoop to share their avid darkness:

one slips it in her landlord's tea. Nothing.
She'd crossed it from her memory,
until she saw the meme.

HashtagScienceMajor censures the levity
in this thread, we're talking 1,1,1-
Trichlorethane, the pocket-poison,

for office and home. One rule of thumb:
the sweeter the taste – arsenic, ethylene
glycol, a *faux*-mushroom, basted in garlic –

the deadlier – like love, or addiction. Sniffed,
there's loss of vision, arrhythmia, and speech
slurs to a white noise, the mind over-written.

A young mechanic from Switzerland dies;
a cortege of alps process at the funeral,
bowing their white heads.

THE SHEER WEIGHT OF TRAFFIC

If destiny is in our faces, it finds
us in a queue, grinding forward
slowly, the jerk of stop-start,
elbows on polished door-rims.

We ride a clutch, repeat a ballet
of indetermination, half-smiles
through lowered windows,
the cooling of idling metal.

Inching up the tarmac chain,
a wrecking-ball of sun pendulums
after our windscreen, flattening
dark trees on a horizon.

Glimpsed lives are suddenly gone,
the sheer multitude. A mum
harangues a rear-view mirror,
an unseen child, a filling ashtray.

TURNING-CIRCLES

Milk curdles at the wrong address, soft cheese runs-off as water.
Hummus on a mistaken front step turns the green of the South,
chillies give-up their furious heat without a satellite location, meat
bleeds into next-door's alley. On one street, a kilo of British Queen's,
on another, Kerr's Pink. Some won't add HP sauce to fish on Fridays;
it has to be ketchup, and no surrendering to the flesh.

I've reversed the turning-circles of Tandragee and Moira with one eye
on the wing-mirror, ridden the speed-bumps to ice-cream tribes
of Martelli's of Portstewart, or Graham's of Drumore, and yes, it's true,
the best cakes are Union-baked at WI, as there's the folding there
for extra fancies. Wakes are tough on my time-keeping, shortbreads
and tray-bakes. No name-badge to tell a Christian name,
though there's those who think they can smell as much.

LADYBIRDS IN THE RADIATOR

Snowdrops are small bollards of light
upended by the mole, all thumbs,
digging in the wet field; crows peck
the road for salt left by spreaders,
a pink morning picks up dust on
the double-glazing. Red dice fall
from vents in the radiator, ladybirds,
fooled by a turn of the thermostat.

Great tits at the feeder scrap on
month-old Stollen. A crossbill
filches seed with a cleft palate,
pale red against dark firs.
The ladybirds creep to cracks
in the skirting-board, warm air
on my toes, the sugar-nausea
after morning's thick-cut marmalade.

HAWFINCH (2018)

The patience of a firing-squad before work: a quiz
of bird-watchers aiming for trees where,
endangered like the fledgling year and hidden
as the morning in a puther of fog, a hawfinch
on a bough: the one true verifier, a silver bill
like bolt-cutters. Silence, only a swish of combat
fatigues as they jostle for a better view, shutter-whirr.

Blown off-course by the night's last storm of the year,
the bird's red colour on an RSPB 'At Risk' chart
not visible to the naked eye, but no less a nose-dive
with no pull-out; the little I know pressed between
covers of a Holden & Cleeves, plumage and outline
clear and committed to memory at the time,
and like the year, passing.

A BRILLIANT ANGEL

a black-belt in sipping water
    from styrofoam cups   no splashing
sushi and chop-sticks are like
    eating in space   there is litter

Instagram is fingers in the dark
    texting at the speed
of sightlessness   night-vision
    eyes   ears   lips   skin

my skin   my billows
    accessorised by rhinestones
I'm owl   in skinny jeans
    shadow in a blue-cotton veil

god save me from black polyester
    pervs   acid-splashers   the demon
of close-family   this   my time-out
    free of eyes   my gaze out

a crocheted window   not bled
    for your entertainment
a mirror   prism   hymen   CEO
    of my own private boardroom

and why the po-face   Pavement-starer!
    there's fun in here   my signal
the same   laughter   from behind
    a   drawn   curtain

CASTING OFF

They bit the cuffs and left them wet,
gave away their jumpers as second skins
to girls. Yes, there were dropped stitches
along the way, involving vodka and police-dogs,
but now, our eldest's face in a carriage-window
waves, showing an underarm of frogged wool
and yellow shirt, bought with his first pay-packet.
Years of knitting our sons from separate yarns,
a click-clack of needles, x-ing in the firelight,
mark a spot where treasure lies, unburied,
equally shared, and soft with careful selvedge.
They made their own patterns in reds and blues
for thickening necks and lengthening arms, as we
purled yardage for their stretching chests, till balls
of colour are lifted gently from our sleeping hands.

TO ALL OUR SON'S FUTURE LOVERS

CONSIDER THIS: those looks you covet, the hair you curl,
entwines many lives, as in any secret, inward family.

DON'T THINK: when you hold him, it is only his hopes you send
to sun and air, we are in the breath between your clasp.

NOTE: when he rubs his forehead as he thinks, or stalks up and down
when anxious, these are things he has photographed, internally.

DON'T ASSUME it brusque we ask of loves you've known. No matter
the lubricious lips, but how open were those mouths, and ears?

ASSUME: this means something, makes memories that whittle him.
Yes, we hear people stay together who hurt each other, unlikely as it seems.

GRANTED: there is the family temper. Don't beat metal when hot. Dowse,
and re-start the conversation later, watch clear bubbles rise through water.

DISCLAIMER: we are over-protective. We held his hand to shield, how else
should we be, but interfering? We are possessive, know what's worth trying for.

CONSIDER THIS: if you enjoy and move on, pass the silver salver left, give
generously, and place a coaster under the glass on the credenza.

THE CAT'S TAIL

A pinch of tobacco for the shaman:
'beware of knives and fire.' He may as well foretell ice,
air, for knives are currency here and fire, survival.

Shiann sniffs out fire with his moist nose, as his tail
to the sky predicts our storms; there is only
my own brown eyes for the flashing of knives.

Bears are plentiful and curious; we eat them,
the liver a shared delicacy, though the men say
too much makes for delirium.

Long nights we huddle together, under the skins
of the eaten. The men pay no regard to me.
Only blue-eyed John speaks to me like I'm no child.

Alone on the island, waiting for first snow
to block the gaps in our flotsam shack,
I sew against the unpicking fingers of the wind:

fur hoods for the anoraks, linings for our boots,
a sack to carry the wood we scavenge. I am given a Bible
for self-improvement. The stories terrify.

South, in Alaska, my boy is made better by me here,
he will have a white-man's life in the capital.
I cry every night to cradle him.

The men hear my moans and shrieks,
fear I'm possessed by spirits of the dead, polar bears,
whales, but here, I concentrate only on the living.

One skin at a time, warmth for the coming winter,
pelt after pelt, I stitch my way home, the smell of snow
in the clouds, a weight at our makeshift door.

We bet on which way Shiann's tail points each night,
casting smooth pebbles from the frozen bay.
If my wager equals any man's, John takes my side.

Words falling with the embers to a murmur,
we get under covers. I whisper to Shiann
not to shiver, and to follow the way of my eyes with his tail.

AT THE AMUNDSEN-SCOTT RESEARCH STATION

Night came months ago and stayed ever since:
the moon, not waxing or waning, hangs up high,
a mothball in a corner of a dark cupboard,
constant as the wind, a feral pet we feed outside,
seal air-locked doors against to stop its rasping lick:
we know all our moods, better than our own faces
fractured in iced-up port-holes. Each day arriving
is minus thirty-eight, wind-chill off the scale.

Our work *is* talk, sensitive in the silence to each
blip or whirr of our instruments, an exact spot
the needle touches on the dial of the jet-fuel
in our generator. We dream in half-colours,
our only sunset a screensaver, for memory.
After homemade hooch (no blow at the Pole
to wipe minds white) and a series of box-sets,
we play a game of who we'd eat first if all else

fails. Irrationally, for a lab full of scientists,
men say the women, the women, the men.

ORANGE

at the food depot, two oranges on a crate.
i don't eat, though i crave them, my lips, cracked.

their colour avalanches in my eyes.
cocaine and zinc-sulphate for snow-blindness.

i love such men that would leave them here.
if I perish, i am my last photograph, bent-double.

i dig in a 100mph wind, snow flies from a shovel.
the gale bullies, i can't avoid its lunge.

our last husky ate her puppies, which is normal.
we boiled her friends, the paws are toughest.

snow-bridges cave in, their thunder is company.
a petrel flew into my sled from nowhere.

young Metz raved and broke a tent pole.
'veh,' he said, dying in my blistered arms.

i hired him for his hilarious English accent.
a climber, glaciologist, i thought him an idler.

he soils himself, i need his sleeping bag.
i am too weak, no, too lonely, to bury him.
his yellow lips, the other colour in the landscape.

DESCENDING, IN READING GLASSES

The wrong spectacles turn me
explorer on my own staircase:
I twist my head to fresh vistas
of wavy, cascading banisters.

I've a neck-cord to free myself,
but enjoy the unsettling. A rake
of steps, each flat horizon, lopes
like an escalator, as I take each edge,

time and again, before it comes in
focus; the bobbing neck of a giraffe,
kissing a tree from high stilts:
mistakes may also be triumphant.

This is boozy, or love: to hop, skip,
jump – and if not fly, then bounce
above the garages, under the eaves,
in a state of semi-weightlessness,

for I have been an Icarus, and crashed:
the sick sense of wax melted underarm,
and the slow salvation of weekly
wing-replacement therapy.

My ankles are white feathers: the last
stair down, the broad lip below the newel,
called a curtail, from the 'tail of a cur':
I have ridden, in full-flight, the beast.

THIS IS YOUR FLIGHT ATTENDANT

In the event of an emergency a poem will drop
from the compartment above your head.
Place over your ears, breathe normally.
Read your own poem first before attending
to the poem of the person reciting next to you.
Familiarise yourself with the poem's exits.
In an emergency, adopt the braced poet position,
ready to declaim when pressed. If you smell smoke,
kneel and follow the line of light poems in the aisle.
During turbulence, do not release your poem.
Do not leave your seat, even to perform verse.
Turn off all electronic poems including lap-poems.
Under your seat you will find an inflatable poem
to slip over your head. Pull on the punctuation to inflate.
For more metaphor, use the mouth-piece. Blow hard.
Thanks for listening to the safety poem.
The bar opens in ten minutes.

TRUE FORENSICS

What survives is love, and jewellery –
a Deposit Box in a tower-basement,
hennaed by heat, gold and sapphire, ruby,

diamonds burnished to a glitter,
scorched from their settings to outshine
blackened fixtures.

Limbs, firm and clasped in life,
burn lightly as a willow-branch, browning
leaves, a wick of fat beneath.

Flames dance upon our face, eyes.
The ring on your finger, an emissary
from a slight wrist of skin and time,

shrunken to a flare of alchemy,
distilled to what remains,
a flaming geometry.

Our fire-licked embrace can't shake
the faithful sleep of a Pompeiian dog,
or a Viking amethyst, sunk in the taiga,

nor that heaven, crackling, thirty floors
above our heads, brought down upon all
our precious, and our semi-precious.

THE DAILY ABLUTIONS

A slew of wet paper on a shiny floor, seeps
between my sole and the leather upper.
I blame students I've seen, thinking
it a laugh squirting water, when I see
the Adidas trainers between silver taps,
a roll of socks, a right leg raised, the foot
on the side of a basin, the other holding
him upright like a ballet-dancer. He pulls
at his toes in the steaming tap, lathering.
I stare, and will myself not to, as when

neighbours shake drips from their cocks
in urinals, a secular ceremony, profane
and prayerful; I can't pee now and to wash
my hands feels simulated. He spits; my own ritual
put on hold, and no good god to reference.
He dries his feet to slip on shoes he'll kick off
by a cupboard given to prayer, the door ajar,
mats unrolled, shy smiles to meet my glance.
I slip by, to scroll the hymn-numbers of HTML,
silent under magnolia fluorescence.

CIVIC WITNESS

Face-front, like church, sat quiet,
in rows, with any victim's family
who have a stomach for it. Nothing
to hear through thickened glass.
Some are jaunty, others inured
by jail-time, a few last words.

A leg, once, thumping a calf-strap.
I can't watch the girls, though
my husband does. One guy fights
legally, to get the chair, a childhood
fear of needles: smoke flows
over his white ankle-socks.

We hold our breath, watching
theirs leave, wedded to death,
us giving them away. The doc
checks for vital signs, a curtain
draws. Nothing but to file out
past the Governor's thanks.

In Arkansas, one time, eight
in a month, the drugs at the end
of their shelf-life. It's no-pay,
a hotel, maybe, if we have
to stay over. Once, driving home,
in the rear-view mirror, a face.

RISING, WITH SUCH ELEGANCE

I can't even name the cow in the field opposite –
Friesian, Holstein, Guernsey? Or know a single thing
about her. She's white and brown, if this helps. Why
does she lean into the hawthorn; is it wind,
or rain-avoidance? Don't thorns prick her side?
How does she rise from lying down, as more than
mere mechanical function, with such elegance?
Front legs flip up like a latch, to a begging position;
she opens her spine, a flex in her back ripples hind legs,
which tip her forward; a swing of the head and a snap
upright, knees totter to the lock position; a twitch
of her ears fulfils her dignity. She doesn't wait for blood
to equalise, but follows through with a skip, a short
half-trot, to ward off predators, perhaps, who,
despite the evidence of their talon-shifting feet
along the branch, are mistaken: she's not today's carrion.
This sloping, from one field to another of a deeper green,
what is that? Are cows curious as to mass and volume,
do they have knowledge of space and time,
the filthy trench of the abattoir?

A BUZZING

fearing

      this orange loses zing
      as I unwind the peel,
      that tea in my cup cools
      before I can swallow,
      that blood withdraws
      from finger-nails,
      that I never again smile
      for sunshine on a wall,
      that the breeze from a
      window I place my chair
      in front of ebbs away.

fearing

      all the hours I know boil
      down to one – the last
      of a party in which
      I fail to ask a girl
      to dance, legs won't walk
      her home before her mum
      is due; that I don't take

wing

      fly to her across the room

bump

      the window-pane, drowsily.

SILVERFISH

Peaty light, a December afternoon,
the same seminar each Monday
after three, knowledge on the desk
in ragged piles. Silverfish eat the starchy
glue of book-bindings. I'm chewing over
a thing I read, and this being
university, people are polite, till you,
backlit like a moody 70s album cover,
break the tedium, silver hair a metaphor
I step into without self-consciousness.

The tutor suggests a tea-break.
My heart is not in a tea-bag and silverfish
are not silver, nor even fish. Stupid
to think you share a similar angle,
our ironies are different; foolish
to suppose I can pan-handle
your thoughts, but I feel something
itching on the skin like silverfish,
who live for years in the sugary
crevices of books, undisturbed.

THE SWINGING OF BELLS

A bronze flick of a belt, drawn through
his waist loops, a snake gripped,
fangs impotent. He smells warm
from the Audi, his nails uncut.
I lift my dress over my head,
naked as the day he held me in hospital,
church-bells hammer the metal hour.

Breathing hard for what's coming next,
the burden of my daily portion, a tolling,
four seconds apart, of the bell's
tongue, rolled back through the swing
of the pendulum. At every vibration
my window dimples, the brown reach
of his bare arm, in my bedside light,

a plank brought down on an unwanted
farmyard litter. Afterwards, I move slowly,
though not so slow as to renew his interest,
leave by the gate to cool my back on graveyard
slabs and smoke the stubs left between
the plots by those grieving and long-departed,
my lighter-flame singeing the hairs on my arm.

THE NIGHT-GENERATOR

choose a view, and limit yourself —
a hospital window,
a catheter, recalls

obsolescence. A square of roof,
eaves of the wing,
a stone castle,

surrounded by forest.
The minor grumbles
of the night-generator,

a speaking friend when 3am voiced
the impossible.
Trees are hands thrown

in the air, clouds move less than pillows
by night,
the bed-sheet,

cracked ice, bog-water bubbles below.
My sweat,
animal,

from denning or sett, grace-notes
of wild garlic.
A nurse

comfortable in his own feet, swishes
in a door-frame;
I say, 'Hi',

only to hear myself; white pills,
beige in the dark,
self-selecting jewels.

TO STARE TOO LONG AT A BRANCH

once
a bare twig staked
at a skinny midriff
now slim and tall
the white birch   overlooks
the garage   inside   the green cage
a red-breast   black eyes   not bothering to chirp
or whatever birds do to project personality
pass themselves off as friendly
when implacable in fact   and me   no more creeping up
on the bird than she stealthy with me
both staring   not fooling
her a second   as I stand   watch
no   more than this   *peer in*
as if her soul wants encryption
in a Nature poem
as if a bird on a branch on a warm afternoon
is even a thing still in this deadwood age
her chest not   in fact   red   the legs
copper-wire   in slant sunlight
her little heart a wheel pulsing in a slow download
while I wait on the deft whirring of blue sky
the twitch of her head
shifts the wavelength   a flicker of the light
I could slay her in a game
of Stare   but a breeze across
the grass   makes me blink first
a tear
reminding
I know nothing
while she has my inner workings
in the small clocks of her bones
of no more interest to her than the chance of rain

TRACKS OF THE NINJA

The snowboard
a finish-line
beneath his feet
he can chase
but not
outstrip

a crow-hood
dark mask
breathable skin
lime flashes
underarm
kingdom of stamping feet

a shallow-breathing Ninja

mokuhanga:
one poison-frog
on his shoulder
to help in his battle
with the snow-serpent
wrapping the world
in a skin of crystal

trapper
rock-hugger   winning
every game of
'Rock
Paper
Scissors'
in a smother of white

enforcer

Ninja   meditating on
                    arc
                              curve
                                        trajectory
              a pebble skipping a frozen lake
                    small shifts
                    of knee, ankle, calf
                    the laconic bird-eye
              kuro-kiri, the invisible one, shrinks
                         to a tiny dot
                    the stillness at his centre
                         schussing to the end
                         of the page
                         full stop

he flies
morphs
loses the property of friction
                                        slides
through fallen fences of white
the moguls of the mind

a frog-hopper foaming up cuckoo-spit
a Ninja from a woodblock
in a mind-game
with the snow
now you see me
          now you don't

at the base
of the run
captured swords
of snow
rattle
in his fists

shake
down
to his boots

LEARNING THE ART

Teeth-marks along the eighths,
sixteenths, measure the boredom,
dreaminess, of a classroom, charred
words in wood, J. RABONE & SONS,
along the foot-length. We draw on
office paper, Dad's knee, a man
of architecture, who joins the RAF,
the ruler for the lines in Rectangles,
a technique learned, made habit.

Hair his razor misses, scrapes the top
of my head, the warm hum of his chest,
a faint whiff of oil from his Fair Isle.
We trace Hexagons, then Circles;
for Faces, his one-third rule applies:
draw an oval on its axis, make three
equal parts, then squeeze the middle
to make it thinner, draw a nose
and you have your start.

Indicate a mouth at the mid-point
of the lower part, ignore lips for now.
Sketch ears each side, where middle
meets the upper section. I'm doing
eyes when I see I'll never be as good
as him, and slip from his knees
in disgust. No word of reproach:
his dad, the driver who would be
a mechanic, the move from one aspect
           into another.

THE SECOND HARDEST THING IS TO SWALLOW

The hardest thing is to bend for tea.
A coaster for the table-top rises
with the cup, to fall, unreachable,
on the carpet. Lipless and rubber-
smooth, I try to lift it between the tips
of my two crutches, but it slips,
a block of soap on a sugar-spoon.

I take to using an old envelope.
On each settling of the cup, a small
world of rings grows, a spread Mercator
of Belgium, Holland, Luxembourg
in tea-bag brown; the new surface
of my map swells, as I raise my cup,
to swallow the Low Countries.

JET-LAG IN OCEAN GARDENS, BRITISH COLUMBIA

A sail tacks into what yesterday was Friday
and is again today. A cedar gazebo has carved
human heads on beaver tails, a salmon swallows frogs,
a bear has a mosquito between his legs. This means
something to me, if I could stop to think.

By the fountain, there's a grey lintel engraved in Latin:
Tuum est – 'It is yours.' Out on Salish Sea,
seaplane taxis buzz English Bay:
grey ocean and clouded sky blur, no shoreline
between where one ends and where one ends.

In the Museum of Anthropology, we acknowledge
we are on the First Nations' land, a concession;
like the snapper who steps across my view
of the ocean, holding up his Nikon by way of apology,
my sight-line arrested, the slide-show of white light
over Greenland, from what was last night.

WAITING AT MANCHESTER PICCADILLY

Platform 3 under *Arrivals*: the digital board
slips down a blazing candle-wick of all
the stations on the TransPennine line:
Leeds, Bradford, Dewsbury, Huddersfield.

A grandchild cranes to see Nana through
tall legs, orbited by a crowd; a couple kiss
for the first time; some lads out on the beer
and curry and always, there is later.

Hens from Stoke blow into an inflatable
man-doll; one vomits, not for the last time.
Nana at the gate, her metal of news
bent inward, pendolino-style.

THE FALLEN SNOW

Didn't it snow every year?
Didn't it used to be ten,
twelve – no, two feet, deep?
Didn't postmen whistle in their snow-boots?
Didn't we help clear the drive with shovels?
Didn't we say, snow was as sure as...?
Didn't we grow weary of snowmen,
till Mum came with kitchen stuff
for eyes and the nose and the ears?

Didn't gravel in a snowball
represent the nuclear option?
Didn't someone fall on ice,
survive on codeine and Ryvita
till an ambulance got in, days later?
Didn't the dogs go crazy,
sheep lose their identity?
Didn't gritters come
too late, or not at all?

Didn't we have gritters?

Didn't we take a thermos to Mrs. Thorneycroft up the hill,
didn't she make shortbread to thank us?
Didn't Mrs. Thorneycroft live up the hill?
Didn't the hill exist?
Didn't Mrs. Thorneycroft?

NOTES

page 12: 'The List of Things You Lose if You Kill Yourself before Sixty' – the acronym SERPS stands for State Earnings-Related Pension Scheme.

page 14: 'The Train Rushes Towards Us with Precious Gifts from Far Away' – the title is from a Soviet lithographic print, 1919, in the Tate Modern, London, January 2018.

page 21: the title is from the Gaelic: 'Land of the Machair, Land of Water'. Hebridean 'machair' is a unique European habitat.

page 23: Ötzi the Iceman was preserved for 5,000 years in a glacier in the Italian Alps.

page 27: 'On College Road' – the poem is inspired by 'A Nun Takes the Veil' by Bernard O'Donoghue.
Carob pods were often the last things left on trees during famine.

page 29: 'The Nymphs are Departed' – the title is taken from this line from T.S. Eliot's, *The Wasteland*, III 'The Fire Sermon'.

page 32: GoMA is the acronym of the Glasgow Museum of Modern Art.

page 35: 'Party-Bulbs' – the title is from an opening line in 'Condo' by Louise Gluck.

page 39: 'Turning-Circles' – in Northern Ireland, Tesco delivery-van drivers are asked to state if they are Irish Protestant or Catholic.

page 41: 'Hawfinch (2018)' – the RSPB reports that under-threat 'Red list' birds have declined by half in 25 years.

page 45: 'The Cat's Tail' – in 1923, Inuit Ada Blackjack is the only female – and lone survivor – of an Arctic expedition, marooned for two years on Wrangel Island. Her wages were for medicine for her tubercular son.

page 48: 'Orange' – the poem is based on geologist and academic, Sir Douglas Mawson's (1882-1958) expedition to Antarctica, in 1912.

page 51: 'Truc Forensics' – idea based on BBC website news item of where no DNA, prints or dental records exist, jewellery being helpful in identification.

page 53: 'Civic Witness' – in the USA, Arkansas advertises for six citizens to witness executions, as it executes its first prisoners since 2005.

ACKNOWLEDGEMENTS

'A Train Rushes Towards us with Precious Gifts from Far-Away' won the Kent & Sussex Open Poetry Competition, 2018.
'The Swinging of Bells' appeared in *The Interpreter's House* magazine
'Tracks of the Ski Ninja' featured in a YouTube video (2017)
https://www.youtube.com/watch?v=OebRHrgtQl4
'True Forensics' appeared in the second edition of Coast to Coast to Coast, 2017, ed. Maria Isakova Bennett and Michael Brown.
'Orange' was featured on John Foggin's website
https://johnfogginpoetry.com/?s=Ken+Evans
'Litter-picking on the Heights of Abraham' appeared in *The Lighthouse Literary Journal*.

Ken's poems have featured in *Under the Radar, Envoi, Interpreter's House, Frogmore Papers, Lighthouse Literary Journal, The High Window, Obsessed with Pipework, The Glasgow Review of Books, The Morning Star, Coast to Coast*, as well as online at https://www.youtube.com/watch?v=OebRHrgtQl4

Also at https://www.youtube.com/watch?v=VEu69wklD3c

Thanks
A special thank you to Eyewear's founder Dr Todd Swift, for his support, insights, and suggestions for this collection; Dr Alex Wylie, for his editorial acumen; and Edwin Smet, for his stunning cover design.

Thanks to colleagues on the Poetry MA at Manchester University, 2014-16, who critiqued some of these poems. Special thanks to Emma Simon for her generous comments since forever.

ᗡᗞ EYEWEAR PUBLISHING